COSTUME AROUND THE WORLD
United States

Liz Gogerly

CHELSEA CLUBHOUSE
An Imprint of Chelsea House Publishers

Copyright © 2008 Bailey Publishing Associates Ltd

Produced for Chelsea Clubhouse by Bailey Publishing Associates Ltd
11a Woodlands, Hove BN3 6TJ
England

Project Manager: Roberta Bailey
Editor: Alex Woolf
Text Designer: Jane Hawkins
Picture Research: Roberta Bailey and Shelley Noronha

Chelsea Clubhouse
An imprint of Chelsea House Publishers
132 West 31st Street
New York NY 10001

ISBN 978-0-7910-9774-8

Library of Congress Cataloging-in-Publication Data
Costume around the world.—1st ed.
    v. cm.
    Includes bibliographical references and index.
    Contents: [1] China / Anne Rooney—[2] France / Kathy Elgin—[3] Germany / Cath Senker—[4] India / Kathy Elgin—[5] Italy / Kathy Elgin—[6] Japan / Jane Bingham—[7] Mexico / Jane Bingham—[8] Saudi Arabia / Cath Senker—[9] Spain / Kathy Elgin—[10] United States / Liz Gogerly.
    ISBN 978-0-7910-9765-6 (v. 1)—ISBN 978-0-7910-9766-3 (v. 2)—ISBN 978-0-7910-9767-0 (v. 3)—ISBN 978-0-7910-9768-7 (v. 4)—ISBN 978-0-7910-9769-4 (v. 5)—ISBN 978-0-7910-9770-0 (v. 6)—ISBN 978-0-7910-9771-7 (v. 7)—ISBN 978-0-7910-9773-1 (v. 8)— ISBN 978-0-7910-9772-4 (v. 9)—ISBN 978-0-7910-9774-8 (v. 10) 1. Clothing and dress—Juvenile literature.
    GT518.C67 2008
    391—dc22   2007042756

Chelsea Clubhouse books are available at special discounts when purchased in bulk quantities for businesses, associations, institutions, or sales promotions. Please call our Special Sales Department in New York at (212) 967-8800 or (800) 322-8755.

You can find Chelsea Clubhouse on the World Wide Web at: http://www.chelseahouse.com

Printed and bound in Hong Kong

10 9 8 7 6 5 4 3 2 1

Picture credits:
The publishers would like to thank the following for permission to reproduce their pictures:
Chris Fairclough Worldwide Ltd: 11, 12, 23.
Corbis: Border and motifs (Patrick Ward).
Rex Features: 26 (Trent Warner), 27 (Scott Teven).
Topfoto: 6 (World History Archive), 7, 18 (Polfoto/Thomas Wilmann), 19 (David Wimsett/Uppa.co.uk), 20 (Uppa.co.uk), 21 (Kike Calvo), 29.
Topfoto/Image Works: 4 and title page, 5, 8, 9, 10, 13, 14, 15, 16, 17, 22, 24, 25, 28.

Contents

Costumes of America

Americans, in common with people everywhere, like to display their personality and their tastes through their clothing. In such a large, diverse, and wealthy country, there is a great choice of clothes to wear.

One of the crowd: most American teenagers hang out in jeans and T-shirts.

In towns and cities all over the United States, people go to work in their business suits or smart casual attire. Teenagers wear their own kind of uniform of denim jeans, T-shirts, and sneakers. Many others wear clothes that express the things they like. Some try to look like their favorite pop stars. The punk band Green Day wrote a song called "Fashion

Victim." Thousands of teenagers dyed their hair and attempted to look like members of the band.

Melting pot

The United States is the third-biggest country in the world. It is also one of the most diverse nations. A wide mixture of people live here, including people of European, Hispanic, African, and Asian descent. Each community brings something new to American culture and costume. For example, many Indian people wear saris or Nehru jackets. Recently, movie star Steven Seagal has helped to make the Nehru jacket fashionable for everyone.

A diverse nation

Many different people have made the United States their home, and most cities now have a thriving immigrant community. In the city of St. Paul, Minnesota, there are over a million Hmong, an ethnic group from Asia. The area called Little Havana in Miami is named for the many Cubans who live there. Dearborn, Michigan, is home to a large Arab American community. Each community brings new looks and different clothes to the city in which they live.

Everything goes with American dress style in the 21st century. Ideas for clothes are borrowed from different cultures and eras.

History of Costume

The history of costume in the United States begins with the Native Americans. Before the 16th century, there were at least 250 different tribes living in what is now called the United States. Each tribe had its own costume (see pages 14–15).

European settlers

In the 16th century, Europeans began to settle on the continent. People from different social classes, from wealthy nobles to manual laborers, crossed the Atlantic to make a new life for themselves. They brought with them the clothes they wore at home.

The clothes worn in America continued to be influenced by European fashions until the 20th century. However, some settlers adapted their clothes to the local conditions. In the northwest United States,

European immigrants arrive at Ellis Island, New York, in the early 20th century.

6

settlers followed the example of the Native Americans by wearing animal furs and skins to keep warm and dry.

The power of Hollywood

In the early decades of the 20th century, as the United States grew in economic and political power, its culture, including its fashion, became more influential. From the 1920s on, the costumes worn by the great Hollywood stars of the day became popular all around the world.

In more recent years, the clothes Americans wear have remained much the same, but the fashions have changed. Fashion has been influenced by everything from pop stars to the space race. It has even been swayed by innovation in sports gear or by youth movements such as the hippies or "anti-fashion" grunge.

The king of fashion: rock 'n' roll star Elvis Presley influenced men's dress style in the 1950s.

Early history of jeans

In the 21st century, no wardrobe is complete without a pair of jeans. These famous blue pants were created for gold miners and cowboys in the 19th century. They were the invention of San Francisco tailor Levi Strauss. He used a tough fabric called denim for his pants. Then he added rivets to strengthen the seams. Jeans were patented in 1873.

Geography and Climate

The United States is a large country, covering 3,787,711 square miles (9,848,048 square kilometers). It has 50 states, each with its own climate and geography. These factors have influenced the clothes that people wear.

The South and Hawaii

In the southern states, summers can be very hot. In Orlando, Florida, temperatures regularly reach 90 °F (32 °C) during the summer months. People have to wear light clothing to keep cool in the hot, humid climate. In tropical Hawaii, temperatures tend to range from 75 to 85 °F (24 to 29 °C). Shorts and swimsuits are a must all year round.

Skateboarders stay cool in cotton during the hottest months.

Alaska

The northern states have cold winters. Parts of Alaska experience arctic conditions. Alaskan Inuit, who are indigenous to the area, traditionally wore clothes made from animal furs and skins. Many modern Inuit wear clothes made from synthetic fabrics designed for cold weather. However, fur trims, embroidery, and beadwork help to give these clothes a traditional look.

The Rockies

In the Rocky Mountains, summer temperatures average 82 °F (28 °C), but the weather can be very changeable, with sudden dips of temperature. The winters in the Rockies tend to last longer than most places in the United States and have more snow. People usually layer their clothing so they can remove garments as it gets warmer. Outdoor clothing such as fleece and waterproof jackets have crossed over into everyday wear.

Keeping warm is more important than being fashionable when temperatures dip below zero.

All-American look

Traditional cowboys were famous for their big hats, high leather boots, leather chaps, and jeans. The hat protected them from the heat of the sun as they worked in the vast open spaces of the American West. The leather boots and chaps helped to protect their legs as they passed through heavy brush and vegetation. Today cowboy hats are mostly worn by people living in the sunny southwestern states.

Religion and Culture

In the United States, people can believe and say whatever they choose. This liberal attitude is reflected in the clothing styles on display on most American streets.

Women can go around with bare midriffs. On the other hand, Muslim women can cover up with traditional head scarves, called *hijabs*. In the 21st century, almost anything goes.

Freedom of dress

The United States is a country of many faiths. The government does not intervene in matters of religious dress, so people of faith can wear what they like, including headdresses, scarves, and religious symbols.

In the United States, you are free to cover up or show off your body. In recent years it has been fashionable to show off the midriff.

Organizations try to be inclusive of different faiths. Some Girl Scout troops encourage Muslim girls to join by allowing them to wear a *hijab*.

Hasidic Jews and Mormons

New York has a large community of Hasidic Jews. They are recognizable by their dark clothes. Most men wear navy or black suits with a long jacket called a *rekelekh*.

One of the fastest-growing religions in the United States is the Mormon faith. The men wear dark suits and neckties with white shirts. Women wear dresses or skirts. These must be modest and show as little skin as possible.

The hippie look

The hippie movement began in the United States in the 1960s. Hippies believe in peace, love, and personal freedom. They often choose to wear non-Western clothes. Indian clothing such as *kurta* shirts and scarves are popular. The *dashiki*, a type of shirt worn by men in West Africa, has also caught on with hippies.

Most Hasidic Jewish men do not wear neckties. They always button their jackets right over left.

Materials and Textiles

Natural fabrics such as cotton, silk, and linen are still often used for clothing. They are cool and light, making them especially popular in warmer regions during the summertime. People also wear animal products such as leather.

However, these days many choose not to wear animal fur after ad campaigns in the 1990s highlighted the suffering of animals used in the fur trade. Today fake furs are available that are so similar in look and feel to genuine fur, there is no need to wear the real thing!

Artificial fabrics

In the 20th century, there was a revolution in artificial fabrics. Nylon was first produced in the United States in 1935. Since then, polyester, acrylic (a replacement for wool), spandex, and Lycra have all become popular. Most artificial fabrics are easy to wash and iron. Because of mass production, they are also cheap.

Road and track cyclists often wear Lycra gear because it clings to the body, reducing wind resistance.

Since the 1950s, artificial fabrics have been mixed with natural fabrics. Clothes made of cotton combined with artificial fabrics such as polyester have a natural feel, but they are easy to care for. Acrylic and wool are often mixed to make a garment cheaper while retaining the softness of wool. Lycra and spandex are added to jeans and other clothes for a tighter fit and lasting shape.

Microfibers

In the 1990s, the trend in textiles was microfibers. These are artificial fabrics that feel extremely soft and hold their shape well. Since then, sportswear has been transformed by the use of moisture management fibers such as Coolmax or super-lightweight fibers such as Tactel supermicro. Another interesting innovation has been Gore-Tex. This breathable, waterproof, and windproof fabric is used in a variety of outdoor clothing.

Modern outdoor clothing is often made of microfibers. These clothes can be light yet still keep the wearer warm and dry.

Future fabrics

In the 21st century, the race is on for more eco-friendly fabrics. American scientists have produced a fabric from corn sugar called Sorona. In Australia, there are attempts to make new fabrics from fermented fruits and vegetables. Some companies are even looking at recycling plastics and old recording tape to create new fabrics.

Native American Clothes and Folk Costumes

Hundreds of different native tribes lived in North America before the arrival of European settlers. Each tribe had its own headdress, style of beadwork, and decoration.

The breechclout, a type of loincloth made from animal skins and later from cloth, was common to most tribes. On the northern Great Plains, these tended to be long at the front, while to the south, they were shorter. Breechclouts were often worn with animal skin leggings.

Some men went bare on top, but others wore a loose, decorated shirt called a war shirt, often made from buckskin. Women wore skirts and leggings or even one-piece dresses made from buckskin. Most people wore leather shoes called moccasins.

Modern Native Americans combine traditional clothes with jeans and modern footwear.

Hairstyles

Caddo and Iroquois warriors had roached hair—more commonly called a Mohawk or Mohican hairstyle—which was copied by punk rockers in the 1970s and 2000s. Women usually had flowing or braided hair. Sometimes they gathered their hair behind their heads in a twist called a *chongo*.

Changing styles

Gradually, Native American clothes became more Westernized. However, people still added fringes, bold designs, embroidery, and beadwork to their garments to give them a distinctive look. In 2000, there were about 2 million Native Americans living in North America. Most of them wear traditional clothing only for formal or religious occasions.

Compared to most modern teenagers, Amish youths dress very conservatively.

The Amish

The Amish are a Protestant Christian group living mostly in Pennsylvania, Ohio, and Indiana. Their strong religious beliefs lead them to live in separate communities, and they follow a strict dress code. They wear plain, dark clothing in a traditional style. Women typically wear a full skirt with an apron, long sleeves, and a cape. Men wear pants with suspenders and sometimes brightly colored shirts. Buttons are usually banned, and clothes are fastened using hooks and eyes. Hats and bonnets are often worn. Single men are clean shaven, while married men grow a beard. Women never cut their hair and usually wear it in a bun.

Something Special

The high school prom is still a highlight of most young people's school days. Girls get to wear their dream dress. In the past, this often meant something long and glamorous, worn with a corsage at the wrist.

These days, there are many styles to choose from, including "baby doll"—short and flirtatious off-the-shoulder evening dresses—and Hollywood glamour—copying the latest fashions worn by movie stars.

Young men still wear formal suits or tuxedos. They can add their own style with trendy cuff links and their own choice of necktie or bow tie. Some prom couples even coordinate their look: the male might wear a cummerbund or necktie that matches his partner's dress.

Smile, please: most teenagers get a special photograph taken of them in their school prom outfits.

Wedding styles

Weddings are another occasion for dressing up. Most people choose the traditional white dress for the bride and tuxedo for the groom. In recent years, however, many couples have opted for something different. Some choose costumes that reflect their ethnic origins. An African American groom might wear a *dashiki*, while an Asian bride might choose to wear a traditional sari. Others might go for a theme. Wild West weddings are popular, with the groom dressed as a cowboy and the bride as a cowgirl.

Dates for dressing up

October 31—Halloween—is an occasion for children to hit the streets wearing vampire, ghost, and witch costumes. On St. Patrick's Day, March 17, people wear green clothing to honor Ireland, "the Emerald Isle." Mardi Gras, at the beginning of Lent, is a big event in New Orleans. There are massive street parades, and everyone dresses up.

This bride and groom wear traditional clothes on their "big day."

Male Fashion

Something is happening to the wardrobe of the American male. Looking good is no longer just for women. In the past decade, everyday men's clothing such as jeans, cargo pants (chinos), and shirts have been given a style makeover.

Male pants now come in different fits, cuts, and colors. It is even acceptable for men to wear pink shirts to work!

New looks

Fashion designers are no longer afraid to experiment with new ideas and looks for men. Top houses for male fashion include Hugo Boss, Kenneth Cole, and Abercrombie & Fitch. Even hip-hop stars have been turning to tailoring. In 1998, Sean "Diddy" Combs set up the label Sean John for urban style.

Bling of the past: Sean "Diddy" Combs prefers sharp suits these days.

Today Sean John is the most popular fashion brand started by a celebrity.

Celebrity sells

Some of the biggest style icons of the moment are from the movie and music business. Style setters include actor Brad Pitt, with his three-day growth of beard. Both he and actor Johnny Depp have made it cool to dress down. However, when actor Leonardo Di Caprio turned up at the Oscars in a stylish tuxedo, many men went for the same look.

Performer Justin Timberlake has become a modern-day style icon.

Face the music

Musical tastes can have a strong influence on the clothes people choose to wear. Fans of indie bands such as the Strokes, the Kings of Leon, or the White Stripes are likely to favor tight pants, old suit jackets, and sneakers. They also tend to relish thrift shop bargains. Followers of bands such as Panic! At the Disco or My Chemical Romance are collectively known as emos, short for "emotional hardcore." The emo look includes black jeans with studded belts and, possibly, body piercings and eye shadow— for both men and women.

Female Fashion

In fashion, women tend to be far more experimental than men, so anything really does go. In the 2000s, there has been everything from maxidresses to microminis.

Many female fashions look to the past for inspiration. Looks from the 1980s became fashionable again and leggings made a comeback. 1950s-style jackets were also paired with jeans.

Vintage styles

When movie star Julia Roberts won an Oscar in 2001, she was wearing a vintage designer dress by

A timeless look

One of the most enduring styles for women is the "preppy" look. It began at preparatory schools in the 1950s and has been in and out of fashion ever since. In the 1950s, women often wore knitted twinsets (matching top and cardigan) or polo shirts in pastel shades. Sometimes they wore giant circle skirts with bobby socks or knee-length pleated skirts with kneesocks. Over the years, the look has become more feminine. In the 1980s, girls wore polo shirts, loose khaki pants, and loafers. In the 2000s, the khaki pants are a tighter fit.

Timeless style: actress Audrey Hepburn was most famous in the 1950s and 1960s, but her style still influences women today.

Valentino. It was one of the most memorable Oscar outfits and helped to jump-start a new trend for vintage clothing. Other style icons who are happy to raid the vintage boutiques are Mary-Kate and Ashley Olsen. Now many women wear vintage clothes because they can achieve a more individual look. It is also a way of appearing eco-friendly. By recycling old clothes, people are doing their part to help the environment.

The latest fashions

Many consumers still want up-to-date designer clothes. Donna Karan, Calvin Klein, and Marc Jacobs continue to produce high-quality clothes for women. In the 2000s, street fashion has also risen in popularity. Urban fashion house Phat Farm appeals to people looking for top-quality hip-hop-style clothing. Juicy Couture designs tracksuits and other casual clothing in luxurious fabrics such as cashmere.

Models show off the latest designer clothes at a New York fashion show.

Work Clothes and Uniforms

In the 1980s, "power dressing" was the favored style for many office workers. Men wore tailored suits and loud ties while women opted for big shoulder pads and gold jewelry. Fashions changed in the 1990s, when employees at high-tech companies in Santa Clara Valley, south of San Francisco Bay—now better known as Silicon Valley—began adopting a more casual look for work.

Following the example of their high-tech clients, many large corporations introduced "dress-down Fridays." On this day, workers could select more casual styles to wear to work. People showed up in sneakers and jeans. The idea caught on.

Business casual

By the 2000s, it seemed as though every day was dress-down Friday. Today casual clothes, or "business casual," is considered the most

It still pays to wear smart clothes if you work in the financial sector.

appropriate dress by many company directors. Chinos, jeans, polo shirts, and even T-shirts are acceptable. However, most Americans will still wear a suit for an important job interview.

New look for nurses

Uniforms for the emergency services have also changed since the 1990s. Early in that decade, most nurses wore white dresses. Gradually, the dress was replaced by a two-piece cotton outfit (top and pants) called "scrubs." Originally, white or green scrubs were worn by surgeons and nurses in the operating room. They are easy to clean and much more hygienic than the heavy coats worn by doctors in the past. These days, most hospital staff wear scrubs. Pink scrubs are usually worn in the emergency room. Blue is often worn in the maternity ward.

Modern firefighters mostly wear uniforms made from artificial fire-retardant fabrics.

Health and safety

In 1994, the largest fire department in the United States updated its uniforms. The New York City Fire Department issued its firefighters the latest in fireproof clothing. The new jackets and pants, made from thermal protective textiles, did not look very different from the uniforms they replaced, but they have significantly reduced burn injuries.

Gear for Sports and Leisure

In the past, Americans enjoyed dressing up for leisure outings, such as a trip to the theater. Today people rarely dress up for anything and prefer to wear relaxed clothing most of the time.

An estimated 450 million pairs of jeans are sold in the United States each year.

Jeans are the most commonly worn item in most people's wardrobes. Sports clothing has also crossed over into everyday wear.

All kinds of jeans

These days, there are many kinds of jeans from which to choose. At the top end of the market are expensive designer jeans. These are cut for a perfect fit and may be decorated with rhinestones, embroidery, or even "designer rips." They can come in different fits, such as "skinny," "boot cut," "slim fit," "western," "high waist," and "low rise." Jeans for the mass market tend to copy designer jeans but are much cheaper. Brands such as Levi's and Gap are very popular because they are good quality, reasonably priced, and keep up with fashion.

Sportswear

Nike, Adidas, and Reebok are the best-selling sportswear brands in the United States. Due to advances in artificial textiles, track clothes have become lighter and more practical. They are great for sports and everyday wear too. Baseball, the national pastime, brought the cap and jersey to everyday fashion. Basketball, especially popular with black urban youth, made tank tops mainstream. Surf and snowboard gear have also been trendy in the 2000s.

Each baseball team's uniform has its own special colors and designs.

Stop the hip-hop

In the early 2000s, hip-hop fashion began to stray onto the basketball courts. In 2005, the National Basketball Association responded to this trend by setting new rules. Flashy, oversized jewelry, baggy pants, T-shirts, and sunglasses were no longer allowed in the game.

The Final Touches

It is the final touches of an outfit that often say the most about a person. A type of hat, a design of shoe, a particular kind of scarf, a piece of jewelry, even the way a person wears a necktie can make a very individual style statement.

As with all garments, the fashion for different accessories comes and goes. In the 2000s it seems like nearly anything goes. Wool pull-on hats called beanies have been popular for a few years. By the later 2000s more structured hats such as the brimmed trilby became fashionable again. One of the most eye-catching accessories of the 2000s has been large sunglasses. These oversized spectacles were a must for celebrities and soon caught on with the general public.

Bling's the thing for these rappers. Chunky jewelry has become part of mainstream fashion too.

Pashmina shawls were out of fashion for a while but made a comeback later in the decade. This time they were highly decorated or ethnic in style.

Body piercing

Piercing first caught on in the United States in the 1960s as a means of expressing rebellion. In the 1970s, punk rockers pierced themselves with safety pins. These days many people have body piercings.

Tattoos

In recent years, tattoos have become popular in the United States. Once tattoos were limited to sailors and working men, but these days celebrities such as Angelina Jolie and Dennis Rodman proudly show off the designs on their skin. Angelina's tattoo of a dragon on her back is one of the most copied designs in the United States today. Many women wear T-shirts that display their lower-back or upper-back tattoos.

Hats off

Until the 1960s, most men wore hats and suits all the time. In 1961, when John F. Kennedy became president, he did not wear a hat. Suddenly hats were out of fashion. Today people think that United States senator Barack Obama might have the same influence on neckties.

The famous Stetson hat, also known as the cowboy hat, was invented in the 1860s.

The Global Wardrobe

The United States' biggest influences on the world of costume have probably been jeans and the baseball cap. America's global cultural influences have helped to turn these simple items of clothing into classics worn by young and old throughout the world.

New life for old clothes

In addition, the United States exports a huge amount of secondhand clothes each year. These garments are sent to charity shops run by organizations such as the Salvation Army. Many of the clothes are shipped to Africa and India, where they are sold in market stalls. Many of the clothes are good quality but are no longer in fashion in the United States However, they can often appear very stylish to people living in poorer areas overseas.

World market

In the past decade, garments from all over the world have become available in United States shopping malls. Top designers from Europe are no longer found only in the most exclusive stores—they are everywhere. On the Internet you can buy goods from stores all over the world. With faster broadband connections, it has never been so quick and easy.

Jeans are one of the United States' greatest fashion exports, worn by young people all over the world.

Ugg boots, traditionally worn by Australian sheep shearers, are now a common sight in American cities.

Celebrity trendsetters

The new global market has increased the pace of change in fashion, and styles from abroad are quickly picked up in the United States. In the early 2000s, sheepskin Ugg boots from Australia became fashionable when they were worn by celebrities such as Gwyneth Paltrow. Singer Gwen Stefani helped to establish a trend in the United States for mixing different clothes and layering jackets and shirts. This style was originated by young Japanese girls from Tokyo known as Harajuku Girls.

The global nomad

One of the hottest looks for the late 2000s involves mixing different ethnic clothes. It's a new version of the "boho" look. However, rather than looking to the past for inspiration, global nomads make the whole world their wardrobe. In true "backpacker" style they mix and match clothes such as Asian kaftans or South American knits with interesting ethnic hats and African beads.

Glossary

Amish A group of Christians living as a separate community in parts of Pennsylvania, Ohio, Indiana, Maryland, and Iowa.

Aztecs A native people of Middle America whose powerful empire dominated central Mexico during the 14th and 15th centuries.

body adornment Decoration of the body using tattoos, jewelry, or makeup.

business casual Non-formal clothes that can be worn for work.

cashmere A fine soft wool usually made from the coats of Himalayan goats.

chaps Leather protectors worn over pants, usually by cowboys and other horsemen.

cuff links Ornamental fasteners for shirt cuffs, used as an alternative to buttons.

cummerbund A sash of material worn around the waist.

dashiki A loose shirt of West African origin. It is often brightly colored and can be decorated with patterns or embroidery.

eco-friendly Not harmful to the environment.

grunge An anti-fashion style from the 1990s that was influenced by grunge music.

hijab A veil or headdress worn by some Muslim women.

Hasidic Jews A Jewish movement of popular mysticism founded in Eastern Europe in the 18th century.

hippies A group of people who reject conventional values and believe in peace, love, and understanding.

indigenous Originating from a particular region or country.

kurta A loose cotton shirt, often collarless, worn especially by Hindu women and men.

loincloth A piece of cloth, usually cotton, that is worn around the hips to cover the private parts.

Mardi Gras A festival that includes street parades, picnics, and other celebrations.

mass market A market (for a particular product) consisting of people in general as opposed to a particular group in society.

mass production The production of very large quantities of goods usually by a mechanized and assembly-line process in a factory.

maxi Very large or long; used to describe long dresses and skirts that became fashionable in the 1960s and 1970s.

Maya A native people of Central America and southern Mexico.

microfibers Artificial textiles that are soft and durable. Their ability to absorb sweat makes them useful for sports clothing.

mini Small or very short; used to describe short skirts and dresses that first became fashionable in the 1960s.

moccasins A type of soft leather shoe with a combined sole and heel, first worn by Native Americans.

moisture management fibers Fabrics that can absorb sweat from the body.

Mormon A member of the Church of Jesus Christ of Latter-Day Saints, a faith founded in New York in 1830.

Nehru jacket A type of collarless jacket made popular by Jawaharlal Nehru (1889–1964), the first prime minister of independent India.

patent An exclusive right officially granted by a government to an inventor to make or sell an invention.

rekelekh A long, dark jacket worn by Hasidic Jews.

roached hair A hairstyle in which the sides of the head are shaven, leaving a central section of hair, which is sometimes spiked upward.

sari A long piece of cotton or silk fabric that is draped around the body like a dress, traditionally worn by Indian women.

Silicon Valley An area surrounding southern San Francisco Bay in California that is an important center for electronics- and computer-manufacturing industries.

smart casual Another term for business casual.

space race The era from 1957 to the early 1970s when the United States and the Soviet Union competed to explore outer space with artificial satellites and, later, with humans.

street fashion Fashion that begins with ordinary people, especially students and young people.

synthetic Made artificially by a chemical process, usually in order to resemble a natural product.

tuxedo A formal suit of clothes for men that includes a dinner jacket and matching pants.

urban style A style favored by people living in cities. Hip-hop style is a form of urban style.

Further Information

Books

Frank, Nicole. *Welcome to My Country: Welcome to the USA.* Gareth Stevens, 2000.

Miller, Brandon Marie. *Dressed for the Occasion: What Americans Wore 1620–1970.* Lerner, 1999.

Senker, Cath. *Letters from Around the World: USA.* Cherrytree Books, 2007.

Watson, Linda. *20th Century Fashion: 100 Years of Style by Decade and Designer.* Firefly Books, 2004.

Web sites

www.factmonster.com/ipka/A0767725.html
General facts about fashion and dress, including fashion in the United States.

www.fashion-era.com/index.htm
Fashion-era is a large Web site with pages on costume history, body adornment, fashion in different eras, and lots more.

www.vintageblues.com/history_main.htm
A decade-by-decade look at 20th-century fashion.